D1406667

YOUR LAND
AND
MY LAND
AFRICA

We Visit

SOUTH AFRICA

Tammy

Gagne

Mitchell Lane
PUBLISHERS
P.O. Box 196
Hockessin, Delaware 19707

3 1489 0004 1 0342

FREEPORT MEMORIAL LIBRARY

YOUR LAND AND MY LAND
AFRICA

Egypt
Ethiopia
Ghana
Kenya
Libya
Madagascar
Morocco
Nigeria
Rwanda
South Africa

IBYA

EGYPT

YOUR LAND
AND
MY LAND
AFRICA

Aswān

We Visit
SOUTH
AFRICA

SUDAN

Addis
Ababa

Copyright © 2013 by Mitchell Lane Publishers, Inc. All rights reserved. No part of this book may be reproduced without written permission from the publisher. Printed and bound in the United States of America.

Printing   1   2   3   4   5   6   7   8   9

Library of Congress Cataloging-in-Publication
Gagne, Tammy.
  We visit South Africa / by Tammy Gagne.
     p. cm.—(Your land and my land. Africa)
  Includes bibliographical references and index.
  ISBN 978-1-61228-308-1 (library bound)
  1. South Africa—Juvenile literature. I. Title. II. Series: Your land and my land (Mitchell Lane Publishers). Africa.
  DT1719.G34 2013
  968—dc23
                                                                    2012041974

eBook ISBN: 9781612283821

PUBLISHER'S NOTE: This story is based on the author's extensive research, which she believes to be accurate. Documentation of this research is on page 61.

     The internet sites referenced herein were active as of the publication date. Due to the fleeting nature of some websites, we cannot guarantee they will all be active when you are reading this book.

                                                                               PLB

Contents

Introduction

Made up of nearly 12 million square miles (31 million square kilometers), Africa is the second-largest of the world's seven continents. It is bigger than Argentina, Europe, India, and the United States put together. The continent is home to fifty-seven different countries, including Egypt, Ethiopia, Kenya, Libya, and the island of Madagascar. Most recently, South Sudan was added to this list when it won its independence from Sudan in 2011. Africa is also the home of the Nile, the longest river in the world, and the Sahara Desert, the largest hot desert on the planet.

When many people think of Africa, they think of hot climates, exotic animals, and widespread poverty. While all of these things are indeed part of life on the continent, there is a lot more to Africa than its weather, wildlife, and hardships. Countries in the northern and southern areas of the continent get cold enough during certain times of the year that snow falls. Huge wild animals like elephants and giraffes roam various national parks and wildlife preserves, but you won't see them on the streets of large cities. Instead, skyscrapers line the horizons of these areas. And although many African countries are poor, some are quite wealthy.

Mountains meet the ocean at the shoreline of Rooi Els Coastal Road, South Africa

One such country is the Republic of South Africa. Most often called simply South Africa, this nation has a long and complex history. From the native tribes to the European settlers who came to the country during the 17th century, South Africa is made up of many different cultures. Sharing the land hasn't always been easy. In fact, conflicts among the different ethnic groups have caused serious problems, including wars.

AFRICA

SOUTH AFRICA

For all its struggles, however, South Africa is beginning the 21st century with both advancement and hope for the future. Since the end of apartheid, the nation has elected four black presidents. Numerous areas of business and industry are booming. Preservation groups have increased the numbers of many wildlife species. With most of these animals living in protected areas, the crops and livestock of rural farmers are protected as well. The arts and sports are also thriving in South Africa. The country is even sending winning athletes to the Olympic Games.

 A seal colony makes its home in the waters off the coast of South Africa.

The Lay of the Land

The country of South Africa lies at the southern tip of the African continent. To the north the nation is bordered by five other countries: Namibia, Botswana, Zimbabwe, Mozambique, and Swaziland. Looking at a map of South Africa, though, the nearby country one notices immediately is Lesotho. The southeastern area of South Africa completely surrounds this small nation. It almost surrounds Swaziland as well, but this nation also shares a border with Mozambique.

Most of South Africa enjoys mild weather with warm, rainy summers, and cooler, dry winters. The southwestern area of South Africa, however, has dry summers and rainy winters. The biggest difference between the eastern and western areas in South Africa is the amount of rain each one receives. The eastern regions see between 20 and 40 inches (50 and 100 centimeters) of annual precipitation, while some areas in the west receive less than 8 inches (20 centimeters) of rain each year. Because of this, more crops are grown in the eastern part of the country.

South Africa is made up of several types of terrain. Within its borders are beaches, deserts, forests, mountains, and plateaus. Numerous rivers run through the country, as well. The longest is the Orange River, which measures 1,367 miles (2,200 kilometers) long. Even longer than this, however, is South Africa's coastline. From Namibia to Mozambique, it is 1,739 miles (2,798 kilometers). The coast meets the Atlantic Ocean on the west and the Indian Ocean on the east.

The cooler waters of the country's western shores are home to the largest mainland seal colonies in the world. Sea birds and fish also thrive along this coast. The warmer waters of the eastern shores offer complex coral reefs. Within them reside twenty different species of surgeonfish, twelve different species of moray eels, and numerous other types of sea life.

Wildlife abounds on the land, as well. South Africa is home to nearly 300 types of mammals.[1] These include many rare species that are only found in South Africa. Baboons, cheetahs, elephants, giraffes, hyenas, leopards, lions, rhinoceroses, wildebeests, and zebras are just a few of the amazing creatures that can be found here.

Even more numerous than mammals, South Africa's birds are another of the country's treasures. There are more than 800 different species.[2] These include the African hoopoe, the grey crowned crane, and the lilac-breasted roller. Reptiles too are abundant: crocodiles, lizards, skinks, and tortoises can be found throughout the nation. Numerous snakes inhabit the area as well. Most of them are harmless, but one exception is the Cape cobra. Its venom can paralyze or even kill a person.

Many animal populations have declined over the last couple of centuries, mostly due to the rise in the human population. As the number of people in South Africa has increased, the animals' habitats have been destroyed. Too much hunting has also lowered the numbers of certain species. Thanks to conservation efforts, though, many species have been thriving in recent years.

Animal preserves provide South Africa's many wild creatures with homes that are protected from both hunting and encroachment. The biggest of these preserves is Kruger National Park, which covers more

FYI FACT:

Many people are surprised to learn that South Africa is home to penguin colonies. African penguins are also known as jackass penguins because of the hee-haw noise they make. It sounds just like a donkey when it brays.

WHERE IN THE WORLD IS SOUTH AFRICA?

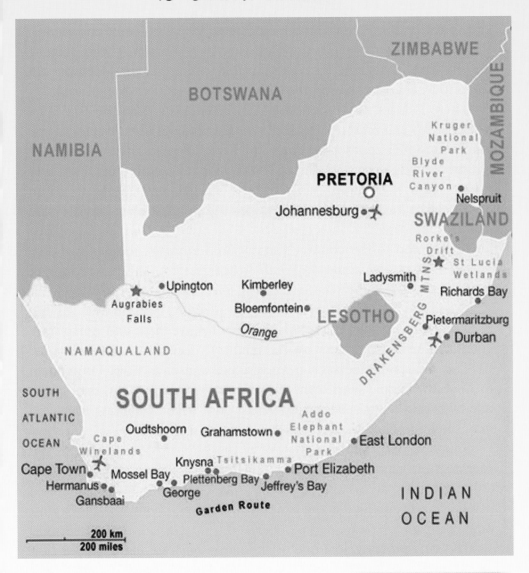

ZIMBABWE

BOTSWANA

MOZAMBIQUE

NAMIBIA

Kruger
National
Park

Blyde
River
Canyon

PRETORIA
Johannesburg ✈

Nelspruit

SWAZILAND

Rorke's
Drift
⭐ St Lucia
Wetlands

Upington   Kimberley   Ladysmith
⭐
Augrabies   Bloemfontein   Richards Bay
Falls   LESOTHO
Orange   Pietermaritzburg
✈ Durban
NAMAQUALAND

DRAKENSBERG MTNS

SOUTH
ATLANTIC
OCEAN

SOUTH AFRICA

Addo
Elephant
National
Park   ● East London

Cape
Winelands   Oudtshoorn   Grahamstown
Cape Town   Knysna Tsitsikamma   ● Port Elizabeth
Hermanus   Mossel Bay   Plettenberg Bay   Jeffrey's Bay
Gansbaai   George   INDIAN
Garden Route   OCEAN

200 km
200 miles

Where in the World

than 6 million acres (2.4 million hectares) of land—roughly the size of Maryland.

People travel to Africa from all over the world to see what are known as the Big Five—buffalo, elephants, leopards, lions, and rhinos. When they visit this park, they are very likely to see at least four of the Big Five in a single day. The hardest to find are the leopards, but some tourists report seeing these magnificent spotted cats as well.

There is a lot more to South African wildlife than the Big Five, however. To call attention to some of the lesser-known species, some tourist sites offer another list: the Little Five. These fascinating creatures are the buffalo weaver, elephant shrew, leopard tortoise, ant lion, and rhinoceros beetle. The majority of wild animals that can be found in South Africa are neither the biggest nor the smallest ones, but they are just as interesting.

In addition to the country's many land animals, tourists can also see several types of whales in South African waters. The most common is the southern right whale. This species swims all the way from Antarctica to South Africa every year, arriving in June and staying until November. They make this journey to give birth and nurse their young in the warm waters off the country's southern coast.

The whales can be seen from beaches and cliffs from Doringbaai to Durban. People who want a closer look, though, can usually get one by taking a quick boat ride. While on a whale watching tour, you may see humpback whales and dolphins as well.

South Africa's national flower is the king protea. Found in the southwestern part of the country, this flower can grow up to 12 inches (30 centimeters) across and 80 inches (200 centimeters) high. Its pointed petals form a cup-like shape around the center, giving the blossom a unique look.

The king protea is just one of the numerous rare plant species that grows in the country. Kruger National Park alone contains more than 2,000 species of tropical and subtropical plants. These include 450 trees and shrubs and 235 grasses.[3]

SOUTH AFRICA FACTS AT A GLANCE

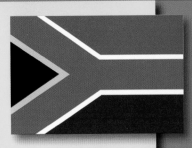

South African flag

Full name: Republic of South Africa

Official languages: IsiZulu, IsiXhosa, Afrikaans, Sepedi, English, Setswana, Sesotho, Xitsonga, siSwati, Tshivenda, isiNdebele

Population: 48,810,427 (July 2012 estimate)

Land area: 468,909 square miles (1,214,470 square kilometers); slightly less than twice the size of Texas

Capital: Pretoria

Government: Republic

Ethnic makeup: black African 79%, white 9.6%, colored 8.9%, Indian/Asian 2.5%

Religions: Protestant 36.6% (Zionist Christian 11.1%, Pentecostal/Charismatic 8.2%, Methodist 6.8%, Dutch Reformed 6.7%, Anglican 3.8%), Catholic 7.1%, Muslim 1.5%, other Christian 36%, other 2.3%, unspecified 1.4%, none 15.1%

Exports: gold, diamonds, platinum, other metals and minerals, machinery and equipment

Imports: machinery and equipment, chemicals, petroleum products, scientific instruments, food

Crops: corn, wheat, sugarcane, fruits, vegetables

Average high temperatures:
   Cape Town: February 80°F (27°C), July 64°F (18°C)
   Johannesburg: January 77°F (25°C), June 60°F (16°C)

Average annual rainfall:
   Cape Town: 18.7 inches (47.5 centimeters)
   Johannesburg: 28.5 inches (72.4 centimeters)

Highest point: Njesuthi—11,181 feet (3,408 meters)

Longest river: Orange—1,367 miles (2,200 kilometers)

Flag: South Africa's flag has six colors. The top contains a horizontal red band, and the bottom contains a horizontal blue band. These two colors are separated by a horizontal green Y. In its center is a black triangle. The Y is bordered from the black with a thin band of yellow. It is bordered from the red and blue with bands of white. The colors have no special significance, but the Y represents the "convergence of diverse elements within South African society, taking the road ahead in unity."

National sport: Although South Africa has no official national sport, the people enjoy many athletic activities including cricket, football (soccer), and rugby.

National flower: king protea (*Protea cynaroides*)

National bird: blue crane (*Anthropoides paradisea*)

National tree: real yellowwood (*Podocarpus latifolius*)

Source: *CIA World Factbook:* South Africa

The first San people lived in South Africa 30,000 years ago. Today most San live as hunters and gatherers in the Kalahari Desert, located in the northern part of the country.

The Beginning of Life

Africa is where human life began. In the Eastern Cape Province of South Africa, archaeologists have uncovered human fossils of *Homo sapiens* believed to be 100,000 years old.[1] Fossils of earlier human species have also been found elsewhere on the continent. They reveal that human life in Africa may go back three million years or more.

One of the oldest groups living in South Africa today is the San people. They have inhabited the area for about 30,000 years. Paintings created by the early San on cave walls and rocks show that they were hunters and gatherers, just as they are today. Over the last 2,000 years, the San have slowly moved north into the Kalahari Desert.

About the same time that the San began moving northward, another group of people came to the area now called South Africa. The Khoikhoi came from the north and settled in the western parts of South Africa, raising sheep and cattle to survive.

Around 300 C.E., the Bantu settled in what is now eastern South Africa. The Bantu were taller than the San and Khoikhoi and had much darker skin. Not only did this group look different, but they also sounded different. They spoke in languages the other groups did not understand. The Bantu kept livestock and farmed the land. In addition, they began mining for metals. They created unique items from the copper, gold, and iron that they found. They used these items as trade goods.

Today, being Bantu has more to do with language than ethnicity. Bantu people can still be found throughout the southern countries of Africa. South Africa is home to the Xhosa and Zulu people. Though not identical, their Bantu languages are very similar.

By the 14th century, several other Bantu groups had moved into southern Africa from the central part of the continent. They included the Nguni, Sotho, Tsonga, and Venda. Each group had its own kingdom. Clashes occurred from time to time between these kingdoms. Many people from these groups still live in South Africa today. While there has been some mixing of the ethnicities, most have remained distinct from one another.

Europeans discovered southern Africa during the 15th century. A small number of sailors had stopped briefly in the area before then. Most were traveling around the southern tip of the continent on their way to somewhere else. None of them made it very far inland before continuing with their journeys, however.

The first Europeans to settle in the area were from the Netherlands. The Dutch East India Company sent Jan van Riebeeck to southern Africa in 1651. He traveled with his wife and a ninety-person crew.

Jan van Riebeeck arrives in Africa.

These men were responsible for building a fort and a hospital in the area for Dutch fleets that sailed around the Cape of Good Hope. The settlers also planted vegetables, so they could feed these weary travelers healthy food. Sailors who didn't consume enough vitamin C from fresh fruits and vegetables during their trips often came down with scurvy.

The area where the Dutch settled was where the Khoikhoi people already lived. Unlike van Riebeeck, most of his men had come to the area without wives. Soon many of them met Khoikhoi women and started new lives with them in the Dutch colony. The couples' mixed-race children became known as Coloreds. This term is still used today for people of mixed race in South Africa.

French and German settlers soon joined the Dutch colonists. Although all three groups were from Europe, they spoke very different languages. Over time, their languages developed into a new language. The European settlers began calling themselves *Afrikaners*—meaning "people of Africa," and their new language became known as Afrikaans.

As the Afrikaner population grew, they needed help to work the land. At first they tried to get the Khoikhoi people to perform this hard labor, but most of them were not interested. The Afrikaners' solution to the problem was to bring in slaves to do the work. Africans from other areas, as well as Asians, became property of the Afrikaners.

Soon the Afrikaners had created a new society in their new land based on skin color. The whites were at the top, and the native people were at the bottom. When the Afrikaners needed more land, they took it from the Khoikhoi people. When they needed even more, they moved farther inland. They decided that their lighter skin gave them the right to treat the black and Colored people any way they pleased. And things would only get worse before they got better.

FYI FACT:

Some Afrikaners called themselves *Boers*, which was Dutch for "farmers."

The Cape Town waterfront is located in northern Cape Town. Although the city had become very busy by the late 1700s, it has grown since then. Today it is home to numerous hotels, pubs, and restaurants which serve locals as well as traveling businesspeople and tourists.

A Nation Divided

By the late 1700s, Cape Town had become a busy seaport. British ships traveled through the area regularly, and they soon began to see the value in colonizing it. The next century brought the area—and the Afrikaners—under British rule. This shift in power caused many changes. The British settlers didn't understand Afrikaans. They also didn't want to participate in the new culture the Afrikaners had developed. They wanted their own customs and language to be used here instead. The biggest difference of opinion, however, involved slavery. The British outlawed it on December 1, 1834.

The Afrikaners were so outraged by the decision that many of them packed up their wagons and left. They traveled over the Drakensberg Mountains, the highest mountain range in all of southern Africa. This move is now called "The Great Trek," or *Die Groot Trek* in Afrikaans. On the other side of the mountains, the Afrikaners encountered the Zulu. Taking land from this group of people was not going to be easy. The Zulu were strong and numerous, but in the end the Afrikaners triumphed. They created their own states in what is now the eastern half of South Africa.

The majority of the land in southern Africa now belonged to either the British or the Afrikaners. This land contained the best farming soil in the region. The states that the Afrikaners had claimed for themselves also contained a great deal of gold and diamonds. The native people who had lived on this land for thousands of years were now at the mercy of the white people who had taken it over.

Just because they had all the best land didn't mean that the British and Afrikaners were going to live peacefully alongside each other. The

British soldiers barrage the Afrikaners using a large 4.7-inch (12-centimeter) gun called "Joe Chamberlain" during the second Anglo-Boer war.

British saw the Afrikaners as backward farm people who didn't deserve the riches of the land. In 1899, the Anglo-Boer War erupted. It continued until 1902, when the British prevailed.

In 1910, the colonies came together to form the Union of South Africa. Following the war, the Afrikaners wanted to keep their Afrikaans language, but the British insisted on teaching English and Dutch in schools instead. The Afrikaners kept up this fight, however. In 1925, they finally won the right to be taught in Afrikaans. The British did side with the Afrikaners in denying blacks the right to vote under the new government, however.

The black population rebelled by forming its own organization. They called it the African National Congress, or the ANC. The ANC wasn't able to stop the white government from passing terribly unfair laws, however. For example, in 1913, the Natives' Land Act divided the country into white areas and black areas. Blacks could only reside in white areas if they worked within them—for whites, of course. Ninety-three percent of the land was assigned to whites. The blacks, who vastly outnumbered the whites, were forced to live on the tiny remainder of land, which was virtually worthless.

Just when the native Africans thought things couldn't get any worse, the Afrikaners' National Party won a national election in 1948. Under their leadership, the new government passed even more segregation laws. These laws became known as apartheid, an Afrikaans word that means "apart."

Prime Minister Hendrik Verwoerd and his National Party were determined to make apartheid the new way of life in South Africa. Verwoerd selected ten areas that he called "homelands" for blacks. He professed that blacks were not even citizens of South Africa, but instead citizens of these homelands. Every black person was forced to remain in one of these areas when he or she was not working.

Verwoerd also passed apartheid laws regarding education. Not only were black children not allowed to attend school with white children, but they were also denied the same level of education as whites. Verwoerd did not think blacks were smart enough to take the same subjects as whites. His opinion was that blacks should only be taught the things they needed to know—such as how to perform jobs for whites.

The ANC—and a similar group called the Pan African Congress (PAC)—organized demonstrations against apartheid laws. These large protests made the government nervous. It responded by banning both the ANC and the PAC on April 8, 1960. It was now illegal to be a member of either organization.

The work of the ANC continued in secret, however. One of its most dedicated members was Nelson Mandela, a young black man

FYI FACT:

At his trial in 1964, Nelson Mandela told the court, "I have dedicated myself to this struggle of the African people... I have cherished the ideal of a democratic and free society... it is an ideal for which I am prepared to die."[1]

A young Nelson Mandela, 1937

with a university education. Mandela enrolled in law school the same year that he joined the ANC. In addition to planning and participating in protests, Mandela traveled throughout Africa and even to London, meeting with government leaders in hopes of finding support. He stated his case to members of Parliament, asking for their help in ending apartheid in South Africa.

Mandela would pay dearly for this trip. He had violated the law by leaving the country, and the government responded by putting him in jail for five years. While there, he was charged with additional crimes against South Africa's government. From 1963 to 1964, he and other ANC leaders were put on trial for these crimes. In the end, Mandela and seven of the others were sentenced to life in prison. He was forty-five years old at the time.

The other countries of the world spent the next several decades putting pressure on South Africa. When the country's government refused to end apartheid, these countries put sanctions on South Africa, refusing to do business with the country. This severely damaged the South African economy. Finally, new leadership took over and listened to the rest of the world.

In 1989, a man named F.W. de Klerk became president. After going through the proper channels, he removed the ban on the ANC and other anti-apartheid organizations. On February 11, 1990, Nelson Mandela was freed after spending twenty-seven years in prison. Four years later, by way of free elections, Mandela became South Africa's first black president.

Mandela served as president until 1999, when Thabo Mbeki was elected to replace him. Mbeki served almost two terms before resigning in 2008. Kgalema Motlanthe took over as interim president until elections were held in 2009. At that time, Jacob Zuma was elected president by Parliament. He will be up for reelection in 2014.

The government of South Africa is a constitutional democracy and consists of three branches: Legislative, Executive, and Judicial.

The Legislative branch includes Parliament, which is responsible for creating laws under the country's Constitution, as well as selecting the President. Parliament consists of the National Assembly and the National Council of Provinces. The National Assembly is made up of 400 elected representatives, while the National Council is made up of fifty-four permanent members and thirty-six additional delegates that represent the nine provinces.

The Executive branch is made up of the President, Deputy President, and Ministers. The Cabinet is headed by the President and includes various Ministers appointed by the President from the National Assembly.

The Judicial branch interprets the laws passed by the Legislative branch and applies them to individual cases. Magistrates' Courts are reserved for minor civil and criminal cases, while High Courts are for major civil and criminal matters, as well as appeals. The Supreme Court of Appeals is the highest court for cases that do not require an interpretation of the constitution—for cases that do require constitutional interpretation, the Constitutional Court is the highest court.

South Africa has numerous political parties—in 2012, thirteen were represented in Parliament. The majority party is the African National Congress (ANC), but the other parties are also strongly united. Before 1994, only white citizens were allowed to vote. Today, however, any South African citizen over the age of eighteen who registers to vote can participate in the free election process.

The Kimberley Mine, also known as the Big Hole, is said to be the largest hand-dug hole in the world. Once a flat-topped hill, it is now an underground mine 705 feet (215 meters) deep.

Economy and Commerce

For hundreds of years, the South African economy was based largely on agriculture. Most people made their living by farming or fishing. This all changed toward the end of the 19th century. It was around this time that the South African people realized that they were sitting on a gold mine—quite literally. As gold and diamonds were discovered within the country, mining became one of its primary moneymakers. The De Beers diamond company was established in South Africa in 1888. It is now known all over the world.

Mining boosted South Africa's economy, which is now the strongest in Africa. The nation makes up only 5 percent of the continent's population and 4 percent of its land, but it produces about 25 percent of Africa's income. Out of all the industry in Africa, 40 percent takes place in South Africa.[1]

In addition to gold, South Africa is also a top producer of many other types of metals. The country is the leading supplier of platinum in the entire world. Chrome ore, manganese ore, titanium, vanadium, and zirconium are also found here in great amounts.

South Africa's mines provide jobs for about one million of the nation's forty-nine million people. Because such large amounts of coal, diamonds, and metals are still buried within the land, mining has a long future.

Mining is not an easy job. Workers must travel deep underground through hot and humid tunnels. South African mines are the deepest in the world. Some descend more than 2.2 miles (3.5 kilometers) into the earth. At this depth, temperatures can rise to over 130°F (55°C). In this kind of heat, rock can shatter like glass.[2]

Traveling this deep into the earth is also dangerous. Miners can become trapped without enough air to keep them alive until rescuers can reach them. An event as simple as a power failure can cause workers to lose their lives. The risks may even extend to people other than the miners themselves. Some scientists think that deep mining can trigger earthquakes.[3]

As the economy has gotten worse around the world, the price of gold has risen. For this reason, South Africa is unlikely to stop digging deeper and deeper for gold. It is possible that machines could be used to retrieve gold and other metals from the deepest mines. Many people oppose this safer approach, however, because it would take jobs away from people who need them.

The majority of the miners live in the poorest areas of the country. Many people travel hundreds of miles to perform this work so they can bring money back to their families. Some of the workers are away from home for more than six months at a time.

Although agriculture is no longer the central part of the South African economy, it is how most of the people in rural areas feed their families. The largest crop in the country is corn. This grain is used to make flour, the basis for many South African meals. Corn is the main ingredient in *mealie pap,* a favorite food of many South Africans. This thick porridge is made with milk or water. Other common South African crops are potatoes, sugar, tobacco, and wheat.

The poorest families depend on farming the most. Unfortunately, they also have the hardest time producing plentiful crops. Much of South Africa gets very little rain. Large farms have an easier time dealing with this problem. They have the money to buy the best farming equipment. The people who own these bigger operations also tend to own the better land.

South African wine is popular around the world. Visitors travel from all over to tour the vineyards and attend wine tasting events.

The most popular fruit grown in South Africa is the grape. One can find numerous different varieties here. Most of the grapes are used to make wine. The country is the eighth-largest producer of wine in the world.

One of the most famous South African vineyards is La Motte Wine Estate in the Western Cape. This company has been producing wine for nearly three centuries. It encourages both locals and tourists to visit the estate, where food and wine tastings, scenic hiking trails, and classical music concerts are offered. Visitors can even plan an event of their own on the property.

Tourism has become a booming part of the South African economy over the last two decades. During apartheid, hundreds of thousands of visitors came to the country each year. Now the number of annual tourists is well into the millions. The majority of people come to South Africa to see its wildlife parks. Tourists also enjoy spending time at the country's beaches, casinos, and resorts. More than forty hotels have been built in Cape Town alone since the mid-1990s.

These hotels also serve the country's business travelers. With the end of apartheid also came the end of sanctions. This change meant that companies from other countries could invest in South Africa.

FYI FACT:

Many American companies have opened businesses and factories in South Africa since the end of apartheid. The first McDonald's fast-food restaurant opened in Johannesburg in 1995. Today more than 97 percent of the food served in the company's South African restaurants is produced within the country.[4]

Corporations like Ford Motor Company and Levi Strauss have built factories in the country. These new facilities created many better-paying jobs for the South African people.

South Africa's unit of currency is called the rand (R). South Africa used the British pound sterling until 1921, when the country began using the South African pound instead. The rand was introduced in 1961 at a rate of 2 rand for 1 pound. Although exchange rates are always changing, in 2012 one rand was worth approximately twelve U.S. cents.[5]

American paper money all looks basically the same. South African money, however, is as varied as everything in this nation. It even comes in different sizes. The larger the note, the more it is worth. The various denominations also come in different colors, making it easier to tell them apart. The rand features pictures of the country's wildlife. In the

South African coins

The colorful paper money of South Africa features the Big Five. The leopard is shown on the R200 bill, worth about 24 U.S. dollars in 2012.

1990s, these images replaced the images of Jan van Riebeeck that were printed on the rand from the apartheid era.

Each of the so-called Big Five animals can now be seen on South African paper money. The rhinoceros is found on the green R10 note. The elephant is shown on the brown R20 note. The lion is depicted on the red R50 note. The buffalo graces the blue R100 note. Finally, the leopard adorns the orange R200 note. In 2012, new notes were introduced which also bear the image of former president Nelson Mandela.

The country honors its eleven official languages on its various forms of currency. Each note includes words in English and two other official languages, which change from note to note. The rand was named after Witwatersrand, the hills where many of the country's gold mines are located.

One rand is equal to 100 cents (c). Coins are available in amounts of 5c, 10c, 20c, 50c, R1, R2, and R5. These coins also bear pictures of wildlife, and in some cases, plant life.

Desmond Tutu is a former archbishop from South Africa. As a social activist, he became well known for his role in the fight against apartheid. Even though he is now retired, he still speaks out about human rights around the world.

South African Religions

Nearly every religion in the world is practiced in South Africa. Christianity is by far the most popular, however. Of the 49 million people who live in the country, more than 36 percent are Protestant. Another 7 percent are Catholic. Thirty-six percent practice another form of Christianity, or combine Christianity with traditional African beliefs. Islam, Hinduism, and Judaism combined represent the beliefs of approximately 3 percent of the population. About 15 percent of people in South Africa practice no religion at all.[1]

One of the best-known religious leaders of South Africa is Desmond Tutu. Born in Klerksdorp in 1931, Tutu began his career as a teacher like his father. His career path changed abruptly, however, when the Bantu Education Act was passed. This new law separated the races in all South African educational institutions. In protest, Tutu quit his job and began studying theology instead. Working as an Anglican priest, he dedicated himself to the fight to end apartheid. In 1984, Tutu was awarded the Nobel Peace Prize for his work in this area.

When the Anglican Church named Tutu archbishop of South Africa in 1986, blacks and whites still could not attend the same church services.[2] Knowing that his work wasn't over, he pressed on. Even now that Tutu has retired as archbishop, he continues to speak out for human rights all around the world.

One of the largest religious groups in South Africa is the Dutch Reformed Church, which has undergone some big changes in recent years. This form of Christianity was brought to South Africa by colo-

FYI FACT:

When Nelson Mandela was released from prison in 1990, he spent his first night of freedom at the home of Archbishop Desmond Tutu.[3]

nists from the Netherlands. Most of the Afrikaners who descended from these settlers supported apartheid. They did not want black South Africans to join their parishes. Dutch Reformists who did not support apartheid were then faced with a decision. Should they stay or leave to form churches of their own? Many of them chose the second option. These new churches welcomed blacks as well as whites.

Christian missionaries have played a large role in the creation of churches, hospitals, and schools in South Africa. Most of these volunteers deeply opposed apartheid. They shared Christianity with black South Africans to help them through this difficult time. Many people see these shared beliefs as a way for the people in the country to unite and move forward.

Another popular religious group in South Africa is the Zion Christian Church. An increasing number of South Africans are choosing to become Zionist Christians. This religion blends European Christianity with traditional African beliefs. Some of these beliefs seem to go against Christian values. For example, some Zionist Christians practice polygamy—having more than one wife. Zionist Christians do not drink alcohol or smoke. They also don't eat pork.

One of the main differences between Zionist Christians and people who adhere to traditional beliefs alone is the practice of medicine. Zionist Christians accept modern medicine, but they think that faith is the best healer of all. They do not believe in *sangomas,* traditional healers who deal with both personal problems and physical illnesses. Sangoma is a Zulu word, but the word is now commonly used to refer to healers from various South African cultures. South Africans practicing traditional religions believe that the body and spirit are strongly connected. Sangomas are even said to be able to predict their patients' futures and remove curses.

New sangomas spend a great deal of time learning about healing from others who have long practiced this traditional form of medicine.

Traditional healers are believed to be chosen by the ancestors, and they spend time training with an experienced sangoma before practicing on their own. Many, but not all, sangomas are women. Both male and female healers use herbs to cure diseases and other health problems. They learn which plants work for each affliction over the course of many years.

What Zionist Christianity and traditional religions have in common is a close connection to the ancestors. Family plays a big part in the religious lives of both belief systems. To these South African people, ancestors are just as much a part of daily life as the living. Being respectful towards one's parents, grandparents, and other relatives who have passed on is thought to bring good fortune.

Other religions practiced in South Africa include Hinduism, Islam, and Judaism. These faiths are not a large part of the population. At the same time, they help make up the diverse South African culture.

Most South African Muslims are the descendents of slaves brought from Southeast Asia. These Muslims are known as the Cape Malays. Like Zionist Christians, Muslims do not drink alcohol or eat pork.

During apartheid, South African Muslims were forced to move from their homes in Cape Town. Many of them moved into an area of the city called Bo-Kaap, which was reserved for them. This neighborhood near Table Mountain has always been known for its colorfully-painted homes.

Sadly, even the Cape Malays who remained in Bo-Kaap are now being forced from their homes for another reason. The area has become quite popular with people coming to South Africa from other parts of the world. These wealthy buyers have driven up the property taxes. This has made it extremely difficult for the Cape Malays to afford to stay. As more and more Malays have moved out, even the look of the area has changed. The bright, cheerful colors are gradually being replaced with more neutral choices.

In Bo-Kaap, the Cape Malays created a colorful, attractive neighborhood. As a result, many wealthy foreigners have bought homes here.

Sugarcane was first grown in South Africa in the 1800s. The plantations required more labor than could be found locally, so workers were also brought in from India.

Most of the remaining Muslims in South Africa are of Indian descent. Their ancestors were brought to the country to work on sugarcane plantations during the late 1800s. While many South Africans with Indian heritage are Muslim, others are Hindu as well. Most Indian South Africans, regardless of religion, live in Durban. While the two groups share both a history and a town, they live very separate lives. It is quite uncommon for a Muslim and a Hindu to marry here.

Most of South Africa's Jewish population lives in the cities and suburbs of Cape Town and Johannesburg. Their ancestors also came to the country more than a century ago. In this case, however, many of them came to South Africa for a better life—fleeing their native Lithuania for religious freedom.

Art is one of the oldest traditions in South Africa. Archaeologists discovered these tools there, which still contained traces of 100,000-year-old paint.

Chapter 6

The Arts in South Africa

In 2011, archaeologists made a fascinating discovery about the history of art in South Africa. The team had been studying a site at Blombos Cave for some time. This cavern is located about 180 miles (290 kilometers) east of Cape Town. The new information came from two shells found about 6 inches (15 centimeters) apart. Inside them were reddish-colored rings made by paint. The scientists analyzed the ingredients of the paint to date the materials. In doing so, they determined that people of this region had been creating art for at least 100,000 years.[1]

The arts are still very much alive in South Africa. The country is home to a wide variety of graphic art, dance, music, and theater. South African shows often blend these different mediums together. Some are even interactive. One may attend a play expecting to be entertained and end up part of the performance.

The end of apartheid opened many doors for South Africa's black artists. One of the most famous is Willie Bester. He is known for using recycled materials in his paintings and sculptures. Bester uses his work to express how he feels about the problems in modern South Africa. Other popular South African artists include Karel Nel, Jacobus Hendrik Pierneef, and Helen Sebidi. Each one is extremely different. Nel gets his inspiration from his travels all over the world, while Pierneef is best known for his South African landscapes. Sebidi has also traveled widely, but her work depicts people from the rural areas of the country.

There is a popular question asked among artists: Does art imitate life, or does life imitate art? The country of South Africa is one of the most fascinating places to consider this question. Here, the arts are about so much more than entertainment alone. During over forty years of apartheid, art was a means of dealing with anger, frustration, and sadness for many South Africans. For some, it was their only source of expression.

Gumboot dancing actually began as means of secret communication among gold miners during the 19th century. The workers were not allowed to speak to one another while they worked. Instead of using words, they began stomping their boots and slapping their chests in a sort of code. Over time, these movements turned into a celebration of the miners' ability to overcome their dreadful situation.

At first, mine bosses banned gumboot dancing. Eventually, though, they changed their minds. They decided that the dancing improved the miners' moods and increased productivity. The managers didn't realize that the dancing was actually a way for the miners to speak out about their harsh working conditions, poor wages, and even the mine bosses themselves.

In addition to gumboot dancing, one can find ballets, classical symphonies, folk music, and even modern hip-hop music and dancing in South Africa. Arnold van Wyk and Kevin Volans have become well known across the globe for their contributions to the classical style. Today many black South Africans compose and perform classical symphonies as well.

People from around the world have traveled to South Africa to learn about the country's music firsthand. Paul Simon, an American musician, was heavily influenced by his trips to South Africa. One of his best-known albums, *Graceland,* is filled with songs that Simon wrote

FYI FACT:

The South African National Gallery in Cape Town is located in the Company Gardens. This area was the very spot where Jan van Riebeeck grew food for Dutch colonists in 1652.[2]

Ladysmith Black Mambazo was originally formed in the 1960s, but gained international fame after recording with Paul Simon in 1986. Today, they continue to tour and record albums, sharing the culture of South Africa with the world.

and performed with South African musicians. It won the Grammy Award for Album of the Year in 1986. The choral group Ladysmith Black Mambazo gained international recognition after being featured on the album, and went on to even greater success all around the world.

Another well-known musician who has been influenced greatly by South African music is Johnny Clegg. Born in England in 1953, Clegg moved to South Africa with his mother when he was seven years old. When he met Zulu musicians, he was drawn to their style at once. As he got older, his fascination with Zulu music and culture continued. As a young adult, he formed a musical group called Juluka with Zulu guitarist Sipho Mchunu. The group's music and dance style combined English lyrics and Zulu music.

Juluka had to work very hard at getting their music to the South African people. The law prevented the group from performing on stage together, because Clegg was white and Mchunu was black. Likewise, state-owned radio stations wouldn't play their songs. If they wanted

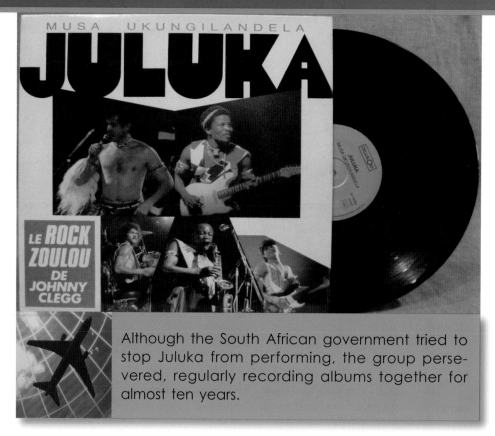

MUSA   UKUNGILANDELA

JULUKA

LE **ROCK ZOULOU** DE **JOHNNY CLEGG**

Although the South African government tried to stop Juluka from performing, the group persevered, regularly recording albums together for almost ten years.

their music to be heard, they had to find private sites that would allow them to perform concerts. The police shut down as many of these private shows as they could. Still, the band quickly developed a large group of fans. Juluka became known not only for their musical talent, but as a form of protest as well.

Simon and Clegg also left their marks on South African music. A form of township jazz called *kwela* (pronounced KWE-lah) has become especially popular over the last few decades in both South Africa and the United States. Kwela contains styles and themes from both musicians' cultures.

One of the best-known playwrights from South Africa is Athol Fugard. Although his plays differ in subject matter, most of Fugard's early works are set against the backdrop of apartheid. His characters are fictional, but their problems are very real. In the 1960s, Fugard's work offered the rest of the world a rare inside look at problems South African blacks were facing.

The South African government did not approve of Fugard's work. They reacted by banning his plays. Even if Fugard had been allowed to produce his plays, apartheid laws would have kept blacks and whites from appearing on stage together. These laws also prevented audience members of different races from sitting in the same theater.

Fugard worked around this problem by having his plays produced outside his home country. In response, the government revoked his passport in 1967. They hoped that preventing him from traveling would keep him from sharing his work with the outside world. He wouldn't get his passport back for four years, but even this setback did not keep him from writing. He wrote four plays during this time period.

To date, Fugard has written more than thirty plays. They are still performed all around the world, but they can now also be seen in his home country of South Africa. The Fugard Theatre in Cape Town even bears his name. Fugard's novel, *Tsotsi,* was made into a film which won an Academy Award for Best Foreign Language Film in 2005. In 2011, Fugard was honored with a Special Tony Award for Lifetime Achievement in the Theatre.

Athol Fugard

Gibson Kente was another well-known South African playwright. Like Fugard, Kente addressed problems such as apartheid, crime, and poverty in his works. Unlike Fugard, though, he did it through music and dance. He not only brought theater to the South African people, he also brought them laughter. He wrote twenty-three plays during his career before his death in 2004.

Not all South African writers were men. Olive Schreiner was the first well-known female author from the country. Her novel, *The Story of an African Farm,* is popular to this day, but she is best known for supporting women's rights and opposing racism. Born in 1855, Schreiner was truly ahead of her time. In 1911, she completed the book *Women and Labour.* It became an important guide for the women's rights movement in her home country, in England, and even in America.

Today, the arts still play a meaningful role in South Africa. They help the people deal with the past and find their way through post-apartheid times. Because so many different languages are spoken here, however, many performances are limited to only those people who understand a particular language.

Hip-hop music has been the first art to combine some of these languages. Black Noise, one of the most popular hip-hop groups in the country, addresses drug abuse, racism, and poverty with its lyrics. These are among the biggest problems in South Africa today.

Music can be heard in March or April at the Cape Town International Jazz Festival. This two-day celebration includes performances by more than forty musical acts from all over the world. More than 15,000 people attend the event each year, which also includes art and photography exhibitions.

Also in March, the Rotary River Festival features live music as well as other fun attractions like dancing, fashion shows, food, and even raft races. This festival has taken place on the banks of the Vaal River in Vanderbijlpark since 1995, and the proceeds go to various local charities.

Perhaps the best arts festival of all is the National Arts Festival. Not only is it the largest event, but it is also the oldest. The first one

Art, dance, and music festivals are common events in South Africa. Many events combine the various arts. Some even encourage audience participation.

took place in 1974. This festival is held every June and lasts for eleven days, featuring art and music along with theater and films.

Of course, not all South African festivals center on the arts. The Boertjie Kontreifees is an agricultural celebration. Lasting for four days every September, it draws more than 20,000 people. The festival features various shows and competitions involving cattle, horses, sheep, and tractors.

For those who prefer marine life to farm animals, the Hermanus Whale Festival offers a unique whale watching experience. People can watch whales without ever setting foot in a boat. Each September southern right whales travel thousands of miles to the southern coast of South Africa to mate in the Atlantic and Indian Oceans. They can be seen all the way from the coast.

Although less than 10 percent of South Africans speak English at home, many adults take classes to learn the language.

Language and Life

South African society is made up of a variety of races and cultures. More than three-quarters of the South African population is black. Most of these people belong to native groups such as the Sotho, Xhosa, and Zulu. About 10 percent of South African people are white. They include descendants of the British, Dutch, French, German, and Portuguese settlers. Less than 3 percent of the country is of Asian descent. The remaining South Africans are mixed-race, or Colored.[1]

Even more diverse than the people of South Africa are the languages spoken throughout the country. The Constitution of the Republic of South Africa recognizes eleven official languages. These include Afrikaans, English, IsiNdebele, IsiXhosa, IsiZulu, Sesotho sa Leboa, Sesotho, Setswana, siSwati, Tshivenda, and Xitsonga. Many additional native languages are also spoken throughout the country.

Over the years, language has been used to divide the people of South Africa. Today, however, the government is making a big effort to break down this barrier. English is used for most business transactions, but special laws apply to governmental affairs. Both national and local governments must use at least two of the official languages in their official business. Typically, the most popular languages of the local area are used.

While most South Africans understand English today, it is important to note that less than 10 percent of the South African people speak English at home. The most commonly used language is IsiZulu. It is spoken by nearly a quarter of all South Africans. IsiZulu is followed by IsiXhosa, Afrikaans, and Sesotho sa Leboa in the number of native speakers. Each of these languages is spoken more than English in South African homes.

When Nelson Mandela was growing up, he spoke IsiXhosa. This unique language is known for its tongue-clicking sounds. The "X" in its name is actually spoken as a click.

The diversity of culture in South Africa has had an interesting effect on all eleven official languages. Each one has changed the others. South African English, for example, now includes words and phrases from other languages, such IsiZulu—and vice versa. Just as the people of the country are joining to form a unified South Africa, the words they speak are also coming together.

Most South Africans are multilingual, meaning they speak at least two different languages. In some areas it is common for people to speak several different languages. In Gauteng, for instance, one might hear five different languages being spoken in the same home.

In general, the native people have an easier time learning English and Afrikaans than the other way around. People who speak English, however, usually learn Afrikaans without much trouble, and vice versa. Many Afrikaans words have even made it to North American shores. The words aardvark, meerkat, and trek all come from the Afrikaans language.[2] Over time, many people have also begun mixing English and Afrikaans. This mixed dialect is called *kombuis Afrikaans,* meaning "kitchen Afrikaans."

The Zulu people make up a significant portion of the black South African population. Of the estimated thirty-eight million black citizens of the country, about eleven million of them belong to this group and speak its language. The Xhosa, speaking IsiXhosa, are a close second at around eight million. The white population is made up of about three million people who speak Afrikaans and around two million others who speak English. The primary language of the Colored population—about four million people—is Afrikaans.[3]

Language was only one of the barriers between the people of South Africa under apartheid. Another was the inability of blacks and whites to live in the same areas or even to go to the same places. Today,

Under apartheid, blacks and whites were separated, even for things like watching movies. Today, people of any background can go to places like this drive-in theater.

people of different races can work together, go to the same schools, and enjoy the same restaurants and theaters.

The cities in particular are now home to a variety of races. Because blacks can now perform higher-paying jobs, they can afford better homes in more expensive areas. An increasing number of black South Africans are moving into urban neighborhoods that were once exclusively white.

Most cultures in South Africa remain separated by choice, however. Many people prefer to remain in the areas in which their families have always lived. Likewise, many people only marry people from their own racial background. Even English-speaking whites and Afrikaners, who

Guinea fowls walking a farm road in South Africa

FYI FACT:

The Zulu have an unspoken language all their own. They create colorful beadwork as a way of communicating with each other. Various colors and geometric designs express different ideas. White beads, for example, are used in *ucu*, Zulu love letters.

often look much the same, have very different cultures that keep their personal lives unconnected.

Farmers and other laborers usually live in the suburbs or in the country's rural areas. Most of these people are poor, living in small homes that are in bad shape. Some have no electricity or running water. Many of the people who live in rural areas have no jobs. This situation makes poverty in these areas an ongoing problem.

South Africa is working to improve living conditions for its poorest citizens, but some of the issues go back even further than apartheid. When the Dutch first came to South Africa in the 1600s, they began laying claim to the land. They saw owning property as a way to become wealthy and powerful. The native South Africans had a very different view of land. They didn't view land as something that could be owned. They saw it as belonging to all the people. Today the people who maintain this attitude are slipping further into poverty. More and more of the land around them is being bought by wealthier South Africans with more modern views of land ownership.

Even with poverty and other problems, many people see South Africa as a place of great hope. Numerous immigrants have entered the country since the end of apartheid for this reason. Most of these people have fled neighboring countries like Mozambique and Zimbabwe. Sadly, the outlook in these places is much worse than it is in South Africa. No one knows for sure just how many immigrants are living in the country illegally. Counting them is difficult since they do not register with the government. The Institute of Race Relations estimates that there are between three and five million.[4]

Cricket is an extremely popular sport in South Africa. The game was brought to the country by the British during the 19ᵗʰ century. Here, South Africa competes against one of its biggest rivals, Australia.

Chapter 8

Sports and Leisure Activities

Despite their many differences, the people of South Africa are very much the same when it comes to one thing: sports. This is a nation that takes great pride in its sporting events. Regardless of their race, religion, and even gender, nearly all South Africans are simply wild about sports. Some people even joke that sports are the country's national religion.

One of the most popular sports in South Africa is cricket. The British introduced this game to the South African people during the 19th century. Many people think cricket is a lot like baseball. Both sports do use bats and balls, but that is the only thing about them that is truly the same. The rules, the size and shape of the fields, and the number of players are just a few things that are different. Countries all over the world play both sports, but cricket is more popular in the Eastern Hemisphere. South Africa's biggest cricket rivals are Australia, England, and New Zealand.

Another British game that has gained a huge following in South Africa is rugby. Just like many people compare cricket to baseball, some say that rugby is a lot like American football. Again, both similarities and differences exist. The object of both games is to carry a ball over the opponent's touch line. Both games also involve intense physical play. One of the biggest differences between the two sports is the amount of padding worn by the players. Rugby players wear almost no padding whatsoever.

During apartheid, rugby was a whites-only activity. It was especially popular with the Afrikaners. The International Rugby Board did not approve of apartheid. In 1981, its members banned the country from competing internationally until racial segregation ended.[1]

Since the early 1990s, rugby has been a sort of symbol of the new South Africa. Today, people of all races play the sport. Special quotas have been put in place to make sure that a certain number of blacks are being given equal opportunities to play at higher levels. As a result, many of them are earning top spots on the best teams.

South Africa's national rugby team is called the Springboks. Many young South African athletes dream of playing on this winning team when they grow up. Kids and adults alike proudly wear jerseys in the team's famous green and gold colors as they cheer them on.

The unifying effect that this sport has had on the people of South Africa is undeniable. One piece of proof hangs in the Apartheid Museum in Johannesburg. The photograph shows Nelson Mandela standing alongside the Springbok captain, Francois Pienaar, a white Afrikaner. It was taken in 1995, just after the team won the Rugby World Cup on their home turf. Both men are wearing the Springbok number-six captain's jersey as they embrace in celebration.[2]

The most popular sport among South Africa's black population is football, or soccer. The British also brought this game to the country. While the Brits insist on calling it football, South Africans use both terms for the sport.

The national team is nicknamed *Bafana Bafana,* which means "The Boys, The Boys" in IsiZulu. The country also has a women's team that

FYI FACT:

During apartheid, some athletes decided to give up their South African citizenship. Runners Sydney Maree and Zola Budd Pieterse were two of them. Becoming citizens of other countries made it possible for them to compete in the Olympic Games. In 1984, Maree competed for the United States and Pieterse competed for Britain.

Nelson Mandela (left) with Francois Pienaar

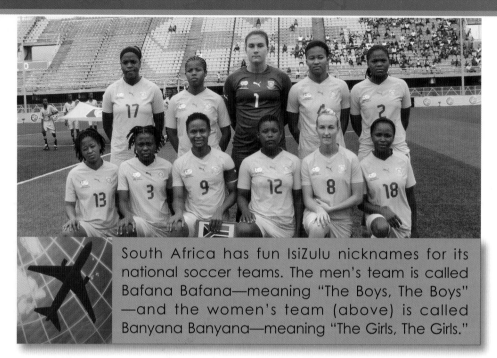

South Africa has fun IsiZulu nicknames for its national soccer teams. The men's team is called Bafana Bafana—meaning "The Boys, The Boys" —and the women's team (above) is called Banyana Banyana—meaning "The Girls, The Girls."

they call *Banyana Banyana,* meaning "The Girls, The Girls." South Africa hasn't achieved the same level of success in soccer as they have in rugby. That isn't to say that they aren't good. A better word for their performance would be erratic. It isn't unusual for Bafana Bafana to win games against the best teams. Unfortunately, they also lose games to some of the worst teams.

Still, the South African fans are extremely loyal. They show up in large numbers to support their teams. One of Bafana Bafana's greatest achievements was in 1996, when the team won the African Nations Cup. Like the Springboks' victory in the Rugby World Cup the previous year, this win took place on home turf.

During apartheid, South Africa was also banned from competing in the Olympic Games. In 1991, the International Olympic Committee reversed the ban following the end of racial segregation. Since the next Games were coming up just a year later, however, the South Africans had very little time to prepare for the event. Black athletes found it especially hard to train. For more than forty years, they hadn't been given access to the same sports training facilities as whites. For this reason, most of the athletes who were able to compete in the next Games were white.

Derartu Tulu (left), with Elana Meyer

The 1992 Summer Olympics were held in Barcelona, Spain. They made history. It was the first time the South Africans had competed since 1960. The Games also marked the return of several other nations —including Cuba, Ethiopia, and North Korea. Due to the fall of the Berlin Wall, Germany was now competing as a single country for the first time in twenty-eight years. In all, 169 nations participated in the opening parade.

One of the most celebrated moments occurred at the end of the 10,000 meters race. A white South African runner named Elana Meyer was neck-and-neck with a black Ethiopian runner named Derartu Tulu. In the end, Tulu took the gold medal, but upon crossing the finish line, she waited for Meyer. The two ran a victory lap hand-in-hand.

FYI FACT:

South African Cameron van der Burgh became the first man to win an individual gold medal for his country in swimming at the 2012 Olympic Games in London, England.

Melktert

Melktert, or milk tart, is a traditional South African dessert. **Prepare this recipe with adult supervision.**

Ingredients:

    butter, for greasing
1   sheet of puff pastry
2   c milk
½   tsp vanilla extract
1½ tsp butter
3¾ tsp all-purpose flour
3¾ tsp cornstarch
¼   c white sugar
1   egg, beaten
¼   tsp ground cinnamon

Directions:

1. Preheat oven to 350°F (175°C).
2. Grease a 9-inch pie pan with butter, then place the puff pastry sheet in the pan, cutting the extra pastry from the edges. Bake for 10-15 minutes, until golden brown.
3. In a medium saucepan, blend milk, vanilla, and 1½ tsp butter over medium heat. Bring to a boil, then remove from heat.
4. Add in flour, cornstarch, sugar, and beaten egg; blend until smooth.
5. Bring to a boil over medium heat, stirring constantly. Continue to boil and stir for 5 minutes.
6. Pour the mixture into the crust, and sprinkle with cinnamon. Allow to cool completely before serving.

String Painting

String painting is a type of art that is popular in South African culture. One of the best things about this art medium is that nearly anyone can do it. No matter what your age or amount of artistic talent, you can create a wonderful, unique piece of art using this technique.

Supplies:
String or yarn
Clothespins
Craft bowls or paper plates
Paint
Paper

Instructions:
1. Cut string into 12-inch (30-centimeter) lengths, one string for each color of paint.
2. Attach a clothespin to the end of each string.
3. Pour your paint into shallow craft bowls or paper plates by color.
4. Dip the string into the paint and apply to the paper. Use a different piece of string each time you dip into a new color. You can press the string down, drag it, or swirl it over your canvas to make a different design every time.

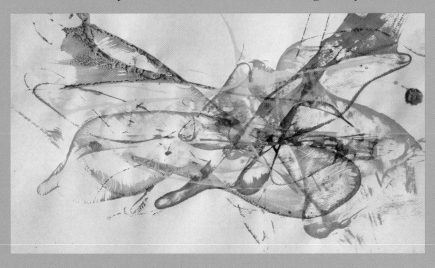

TIMELINE

B.C.E.

ca. 28,000   The San people inhabit the area that is now South Africa.

C.E.

ca. 1   The Khoikhoi come to South Africa.

ca. 300   The Bantu settle in what is now eastern South Africa.

1300s   The Nguni, Sotho, Tsonga, and Venda kingdoms settle in South Africa.

1400s   Europeans discover southern Africa.

1651   The Dutch East India Company sends Jan van Riebeeck to southern Africa.

1600s   The Netherlands, and later France and Germany, colonize the area. They develop a new language called Afrikaans. It combines words from their various native languages, with the majority of words of Dutch origin.

1795   Britain captures South Africa from the Netherlands, but the Dutch later regain control; the British finally seize the area in 1806.

1808   The first cricket match is played in Cape Town.

1834   On December 1, Britain outlaws slavery. Many Afrikaners then leave the area in the Great Trek, heading east and establishing their own republics.

Late 1800s   Gold and diamonds are discovered within the country's borders.

1888   The De Beers diamond company is established in South Africa.

1899   The British and the Afrikaners fight in the Anglo-Boer War, which lasts until the 1902 British victory.

1910   The Cape, Natal, Transvaal, and Orange River Colonies come together to form the Union of South Africa.

1912   The African National Congress (ANC) is formed to represent the interests of South Africa's black population.

1913   The Natives' Land Act divides the country into white areas and black areas.

1921   South Africa begins using the South African pound instead of the British pound sterling as currency.

1948   The Afrikaners' party wins a national election. The new government passes more segregation laws, known as apartheid.

1959   The Pan African Congress (PAC) is formed, protesting and campaigning against apartheid laws.

1960s   Playwright Athol Fugard writes about the problems South African blacks are facing. The government reacts by banning his plays.

1960	On April 8, the government bans both the ANC and the PAC.
1961	The rand is introduced, replacing the pound as the unit of currency.
1963 to 1964	Nelson Mandela and other ANC leaders are put on trial. Mandela and seven others are sentenced to life in prison.
1967	The South African government revokes Fugard's passport to prevent him from producing his plays in other parts of the world.
1981	The International Rugby Board bans South Africa from competing internationally until racial segregation ends.
1984	Desmond Tutu is awarded the Nobel Peace Prize for his work in fighting apartheid. Sydney Maree competes for the United States and Zola Budd Pieterse competes for Britain in the 1984 Olympics.
1986	The Anglican Church names Desmond Tutu archbishop of South Africa.
1989	F.W. de Klerk becomes president. He removes the ban on the ANC and other anti-apartheid organizations.
1990	Nelson Mandela is freed after spending twenty-seven years in prison.
1991	The International Olympic Committee reverses its ban on South Africa.
1994	Mandela becomes South Africa's first black president by free elections.
1995	The Springboks win the Rugby World Cup.
1996	South Africa wins the African Nations Cup in soccer.
1999	Thabo Mbeki is elected president.
2005	*Tsotsi,* a movie based on Fugard's novel of the same name, wins an Academy Award for Best Foreign Language Film.
2008	President Mbeki resigns, Kgalema Motlanthe takes over as president.
2009	Jacob Zuma is elected president by Parliament.
2010	South Africa hosts the World Cup.
2011	Archaeologists studying Blombos Cave learn that the people of this area have been creating art for at least 100,000 years. Fugard is honored with a Special Tony Award for Lifetime Achievement in the Theatre.

CHAPTER NOTES

Chapter 1. The Lay of the Land

1. Don E. Wilson and DeeAnn M. Reeder, Eds., *Mammal Species of the World,* 3rd edition. Smithsonian National Museum of Natural History, http://www.vertebrates.si.edu/msw/mswcfapp/msw/index.cfm

2. World Institute for Conservation & Environment, "Birds of South Africa," http://www.birdlist.org/south_africa.htm

3. Frommer's, "Introduction to Kruger National Park," http://www.frommers.com/destinations/krugernationalpark/2456010001.html

Chapter 2. The Beginning of Life

1. Robert Sanders, *UC Berkeley News,* "160,000-year-old fossilized skulls uncovered in Ethiopia are oldest anatomically modern humans," June 11, 2003, http://www.berkeley.edu/news/media/releases/2003/06/11_idaltu.shtml

Chapter 3. A Nation Divided

1. United Nations: Nelson Mandela International Day, "Speaking out for Justice," http://www.un.org/en/events/mandeladay/inhiswords.shtml

Chapter 4. Economy and Commerce

1. Timothy Kalyegira, Africa Almanac, "Top 100 Africans of the Year 2001."

2. Nicholas Wadhams, *National Geographic News,* "World's Deepest Mines Highlight Risks of New Gold Rush," November 6, 2007, http://news.nationalgeographic.com/news/2007/11/071106-africa-mine.html

3. Richard A. Lovett, *National Geographic News,* "Coal Mining Causing Earthquakes, Study Says," January 3, 2007, http://news.nationalgeographic.com/news/2007/01/070103-mine-quake.html

4. Joburg Tourism, "McDonalds," http://www.joburgtourism.com/things-to-do/restaurants/general/johannesburg-city/mcdonalds-JSRES1095

5. XE.com, "Currency Converter," http://www.xe.com/?c=ZAR

Chapter 5. South African Religions

1. Central Intelligence Agency, *The World Factbook,* "South Africa,"

https://www.cia.gov/library/publications/the-world-factbook/geos/sf.html

2. NobelPrize.org, "Desmond Tutu—Biography," http://www.nobelprize.org/nobel_prizes/peace/laureates/1984/tutu-bio.html

3. Janine Erasmus, "Mandela: 20 years of freedom," SouthAfrica.info, February 11, 2010, http://www.southafrica.info/about/history/20years.htm

Chapter 6. The Arts in South Africa

1. Amina Khan, *Los Angeles Times,* "Artifacts Indicate a 100,000-Year-Old Art Studio," October 14, 2011, http://articles.latimes.com/2011/oct/14/science/la-sci-ancient-paint-20111014

2. City of Cape Town, "The Company's Garden," http://www.capetown.gov.za/en/parks/Pages/TheCompanysGarden.aspx

Chapter 7. Language and Life

1. Central Intelligence Agency, *The World Factbook,* "South Africa," https://www.cia.gov/library/publications/the-world-factbook/geos/sf.html

2. TranslationDirectory.com, "English words of Afrikaans origin," http://www.translationdirectory.com/glossaries/glossary153.htm

3. SouthAfrica.info, "South Africa's population," May 12, 2012, http://www.southafrica.info/about/people/population.htm

4. Caroline Hawley, BBC News, "Refugees Flee South Africa Attacks," May 16, 2008, http://news.bbc.co.uk/2/hi/africa/7404351.stm

Chapter 8. Sports and Leisure Activities

1. South African History Online, "International Rugby World Cup Timeline 1983-2011," http://www.sahistory.org.za/topic/international-rugby-world-cup-timeline-1983-2011

2. SouthAfrica.info, "Rugby, football—and a nation united," July 9, 2010, http://www.southafrica.info/2010/uniting.htm

Books

Brett, Michael, et. al. *South Africa.* New York: DK Publishing, 2011.

Downing, David. *Apartheid in South Africa.* Chicago, IL: Heinemann-Raintree, 2004.

Kramer, Ann. *Mandela: The Rebel Who Led His Nation to Freedom.* Washington, DC: National Geographic, 2008.

Sheen, Barbara. *Foods of South Africa.* Farmington Hills, MI: KidHaven Press, 2012.

On the Internet

Dugger, Celia W. "South African Children Push for Better Schools." *The New York Times,* September 24, 2009. http://www.nytimes.com/2009/09/25/world/africa/25safrica. html

Kermeliotis, Teo. "'Zambezia': 3D Animation Puts South Africa Film in the Picture." CNN, July 26, 2012. http://www.cnn.com/2012/07/26/showbiz/zambezia-animation-south-africa/index.html

Kids Can Travel: "Whale Watching in South Africa," http://www.kidscantravel.com/thingstodofamily/whalewatchingsouthafrica/plan/index.html

Kids World Travel Guide: "South Africa for Kids," http://www.kids-world-travel-guide.com/south-africa-for-kids.html

National Geographic Kids: "South African Wildlife," http://kids.nationalgeographic.com/kids/photos/south-african-wildlife/

PBS Kids Go!: *Africa For Kids,* "Ngaka Maseko High, Winterveldt, South Africa," http://pbskids.org/africa/myworld/ngaka.html

Time for Kids: Around the World, "South Africa," http://www.timeforkids.com/destination/south-africa

WORKS CONSULTED

African Success: People Changing the Face of Africa. "Biography of Gibson Kente." October 18, 2008. http://www.africansuccess.org/visuFiche.php?id=566&lang=en

Associated Press. "Van der Burgh delivers Olympic gold to Safrica." July 29, 2012. http://sportsillustrated.cnn.com/2012/olympics/swimming/wires/07/29/2090.ap.oly.swm.south.africa.s.gold/index.html

Cosi, Roberta, et. al. *National Geographic Traveler: South Africa.* Washington, DC: National Geographic, 2009.

De Bruyn, Pippa. *Frommer's South Africa.* Hoboken, New Jersey: Wiley Publishing, 2011.

Higginbottom, Karen, and Narelle King. "The Live Trade in Freeranging Wildlife Within South Africa, and Implications for Australia." Wildlife Tourism International (Australian Government), December 2006. https://rirdc.infoservices.com.au/downloads/06-046

JohnnyClegg.com: "Johnny Clegg Biography and Awards," http://www.johnnyclegg.com/biog.html

Kalyegira, Timothy. "Top 100 Africans of the Year 2001." Africa Almanac. http://www.africaalmanac.com/top100africans.html

National Geographic: "South Africa Facts," http://travel.nationalgeographic.com/travel/countries/south-africa-facts/

Parker, Jennifer Leigh. "Hunting For Gold In World's Deepest Mine." CNBC, August 30, 2011. http://www.cnbc.com/id/44279553/Hunting_For_Gold_In_World_s_Deepest_Mine

Sanders, Robert. "160,000-year-old fossilized skulls uncovered in Ethiopia are oldest anatomically modern humans." *UC Berkeley News,* June 11, 2003. http://www.berkeley.edu/news/media/releases/2003/06/11_idaltu.shtml

South African Government Information: "Constitution of the Republic of South Africa, 1996," http://www.info.gov.za/documents/constitution/

South African Tourism: "Gumboot Dancing," http://www.southafrica.net/sat/content/en/us/full-article?oid=20921&sn=Detail&pid=7014.

U.S. Department of Commerce: "Doing Business in South Africa—2011 Country Commercial Guide for U.S. Companies," http://export.gov/southafrica/build/groups/public/@bg_za/documents/webcontent/bg_za_034197.pdf

Warne, Kennedy. "South Africa's Teeming Seas." National Geographic (republished from the pages of *National Geographic* magazine). http://science.nationalgeographic.com/science/earth/surface-of-the-earth/south-african-coast/

GLOSSARY

agriculture (AG-ri-kul-cher): the production of crops or livestock

apartheid (uh-PART-heyt): a system that separates people by race or class

archbishop (arch-BISH-up): a clergy member of the highest rank

denomination (dih-nom-uh-NEY-shun): a value of money

encroach (en-KROHCH): to move beyond proper limits, taking resources belonging to another individual or group

Homo sapiens (HOH-moh SEY-pee-uns): the species of primates to which modern human beings belong

immigrant (IM-i-gruhnt): a person who comes from one country to live permanently in another

missionary (MISH-uh-ner-ee): a person sent by a church to an area to offer help such as medical care or education to the people

sanction (SANGK-shun): an economic or military measure taken by one country or group of countries to pressure another country to comply with an international law

sangoma (san-GO-mah): a traditional Zulu healer who deals with both personal problems and physical illness

scurvy (SKUR-vee): a disease caused by a lack of vitamin C

segregation (seg-ri-GEY-shun): the act of separating people by race or class

PHOTO CREDITS: Cover, All photos—cc-by-sa-2.0. Every effort has been made to locate all copyright holders of material used in this book. If any errors or omissions have occurred, corrections will be made in future editions of the book.

Tammy Gagne is the author of numerous books for both adults and children, including *The Nile River* and *We Visit Madagascar* for Mitchell Lane Publishers. One of her favorite pastimes is visiting schools to speak to children about the writing process. She resides in northern New England with her husband, son, and a menagerie of animals.